able of Contents

W9-BGG-678

continued on next page

continued from previous page

STEP FOUR: FRACTIONS

STEP FIVE: DECIMALS

  ©1983, Instructional Fai

ddition

nd pairs of numbers whose sum is **48.**

36	24	24	11	43
18	30	17	37	5
25	23	31	22	51
29	8	40	26	28
19	35	13	34	20

lso find pairs of numbers whose sum is **54.**

Begin Step 1 Addition and Subtraction

1

Number Puzzl

Add going across.
Subtract going down.

321	+	156	+	284	=	
—		—		—		—
58	+	39	+	73	=	
—		—		—		—
14	+	85	+	102	=	
=		=		=		=
	+		+		=	

ɔrossnumber Puzzle

ɔnd the sums and differences. Then write ɔur answers in the cross number puzzle ɔelow.

ɔcross:

a	1958	d	789	e	47495
	+1234		—384		—47469

down:

g	4897	i	3201	a	1687
	+3707		—1354		+1800

100	c	5555	f	347	h	24
+6		+3946		+340		+24

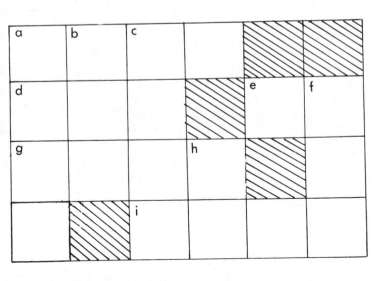

3

Number Puzzl

Add going across.
Subtract going down.

625	+	107	+	211	=
−		−		−	−
436	+	28	+	65	=
−		−		−	−
109	+	17	+	83	=
=		=		=	=
	+		+		=

The Homework Booklet

Number Puzzle

Perform the operations as indicated.

415	+	362	−	194	=	
+		+		+		+
277	+	409	−	384	=	
−		−		−		−
306	+	211	−	186	=	
=		=		=		=
	+		−		=	

5

How Far?

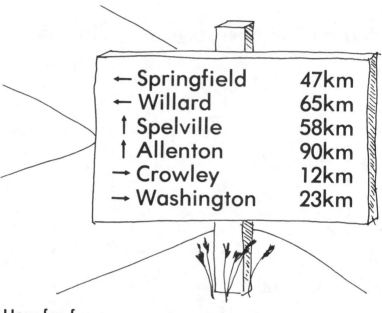

←	Springfield	47km
←	Willard	65km
↑	Spelville	58km
↑	Allenton	90km
→	Crowley	12km
→	Washington	23km

How far from:

Willard to Springfield?	Willard to Crowley?	Spelville to Allenton?
_____ km	_____ km	_____ km
Washington to Crowley?	Willard to Washington?	Crowley to Springfield?
_____ km	_____ km	_____ km

6

igure the Distance

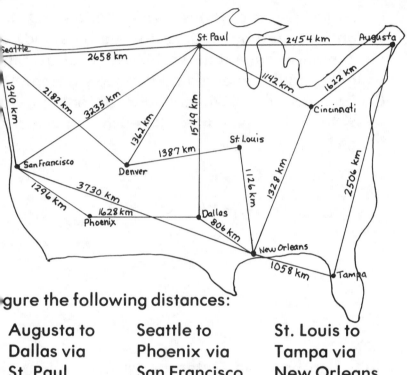

gure the following distances:

Augusta to Dallas via St. Paul	Seattle to Phoenix via San Francisco	St. Louis to Tampa via New Orleans
2454 km +1549 ――――― km	km ――――― km	km ――――― km

St. Paul to New Orleans via Dallas	San Francisco to Tampa via New Orleans	Augusta to New Orleans via Cincinnati
km ――――― km	km ――――― km	km ――――― km

7

Weighty Problem:

Dr. Albert Guthrie who is a veterinarian finds th
weight of a dog by holding it while he stands o
an ordinary bathroom scale. He subtracts hi
weight from the total to find the dog's weight. D
Guthrie weighs 176 pounds. Based on th
following totals, how much do each of these dog
weigh?

Sam	Caesar	Barker	Fluffy
234	218	227	210

Sally Henshaw, Dr. Guthrie's partner, weighs 11
pounds. How much do each of these dogs weigh?

Corkie	Sheppie	Binky	Wagger
159	147	130	175

8

Overweight?

Maria weighs 42 kilograms. Her friend, Andrea, weighs 58 kilograms. They figure for their height and age, they should each weigh 50 kilos. Figure how much Maria must gain.

Figure how much Andrea must lose.

Mrs. Salinas' family used to tease her because she was over-weight. Finally she decided to lose 20 kilograms. Her weight goal is 67 kg. Figure how much Mrs. Salinas now weighs.

Dyane weighs 47 kg. She wants to weigh 55 kg which is what her sister, Vila, now weighs. Figure how much Dyane plans to gain.

9

Circus Clow

Koko, the oldest clown in the circus, joined th circus when he was 11 years old. He is now 8 Everyone is making plans for a diamond jubile when Koko celebrates 75 years with the circu Figure how long before the big celebration.

Koko says that he has averaged 5,000 miles per year since joining the circus. Figure how many miles Koko has already traveled with the circus.

It takes 4 yards of fabric for each clown suit. Kok wears out 3 clown suits per year. Figure ho much fabric has been used in Koko's suits over th years.

Multiplication

Begin Step 2

10

Circus Acrobat

Methuselah Mullegan, the circus acrobat, joined the circus when he was 13 years old. He has been with the circus for 76 years. Figure Methuselah's age.

Methuselah has averaged 8 shows per week since joining the circus. At 52 weeks per year, figure how many shows he has done.

In each show, Methuselah walks a distance of 100 meters across a high wire 15 meters above the ground. Figure how many kilometers Methuselah has walked above the ground.

11

Pounds Plu

Vonda weighs four times as much as her little sister, Pat. Pat weighs 21 pounds. Figure how much Vonda weighs.

Eddie weighs 93 pounds. His brother, Ron, weighs 84 pounds. Their father weighs as much as both brothers. Figure how much their father weighs.

Jim wants to gain enough weight so that he weighs as much as his mother. Jim's mother weighs 115 pounds. Jim now weighs 97 pounds. Figure how much he plans to gain.

12

Number Table

Complete the table.

X		4			7
9	72			81	
				54	
	56		42		
8					
5			30		

13

Pick a Pai

Find pairs of numbers whose product is 4(

10	4	8	20	9
5	9	5	2	4
12	3	6	18	6
40	1	6	36	8
10	4	9	1	5

Also find pairs of numbers whose produ
is 36.

14

Number Table

Complete the table.

X	9			2	
	45		40		
8		32			48
0					0
				14	42
1					

15

©1983, Instructional Fair, Inc.

Crossnumber Puzzle

Find the products.
Then write your answers in the cross number
puzzle below.

across:

^{a} 76	^{c} 7	^{e} 63	^{f} 36	^{h} 85
X12	X7	X3	X18	X5

down:

^{b} 14	^{c} 8	^{d} 110	^{e} 13	^{g} 11
X14	X6	X9	X14	X4

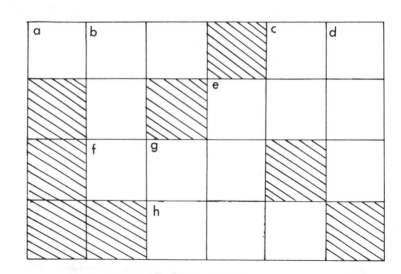

Multiplication

Find the products.

48 X2 — 96	72 X8 —	35 X9 —	45 X4 —

42 X3 —	57 X6 —	36 X8 —	65 X3 —

72 X9 —	45 X3 —	28 X7 —	87 X5 —

53 X4 —	42 X5 —	81 X7 —	91 X3 —

76 X5 —	48 X2 —	89 X3 —	47 X3 —

17

Multiplicatio

Find the products.

We did this one for you

| 675 |
| X3 |
| 2,025 |

487
X6

623
X4

942
X6

425
X7

287
X6

243
X4

496
X2

475
X2

264
X3

434
X6

156
X7

272
X6

306
X7

344
X9

The Homework Booklet

Number Sentences

Fill in the blanks so that all the number sentences are true.

2			14	X	8	=	
X			+				
6	X	16	=				
=			=				
				=	21	+	
				X		X	
		8	6	5			
		X	=	=			
	X	18	=				
X	=						
15		=	8	X			
=							

Multiplicatio

Find the products.

Here's an example

```
    23
   X58
   184
   115
 1,334
```

```
    46
   X98
```

```
    89
   X53
```

```
    27
   X46
```

```
    54
   X37
```

```
    48
   X26
```

```
    93
   X71
```

```
    67
   X58
```

```
    68
   X68
```

```
    51
   X76
```

```
    34
   X48
```

```
    62
   X89
```

20

Multiplication

Find the products.

36 X4	452 X3	6489 X9
54 X3	368 X2	6751 X4
48 X28	251 X64	4381 X72
78 X47	524 X47	5483 X91

Multiplicatio

Find the products.

How to start

648	375	926
X17	X68	X84
4536		
648		
11,016		

498	836	547
X29	X30	X49

560	213	605
X51	X42	X58

743	649	711
X58	X34	X87

The Homework Booklet

Multiplication

Find the products.

193 X76 1158 1351 14,668	749 X42	675 X23

657 X43	238 X54	326 X47

421 X18	317 X29	254 X78

487 X56	492 X36	389 X26

23

Multiplicatio

Find the products.

```
    702
  X415
   3510
    702
  2808
291,330
```

```
    568
  X172
```

```
    886
  X359
```

```
    450
  X217
```

```
    732
  X648
```

```
    598
  X392
```

Multiplication

Find the products.

```
   172              539
 X154            X277
   688
   860
   172
26,488
```

```
   658              427
 X431            X793
```

```
   395              648
 X235            X579
```

Homework Booklet   ©1983, Instructional Fair, Inc.

Multiplicatio

Find the products.

an example

5284		7334
X31		X28
5284		
15852		
163,804		

6920   4372
X84   X96

2432   3583
X12   X49

The Homework Booklet   ©1983, Instructional Fair, In

Multiplication

Find the products.

```
  2075          6724
   X87           X16
 14525
 16600
180,525
```

```
 7926          5381
  X40           X64
```

```
 4562          2831
  X35           X52
```

Multiplication

Find the products.

```
      5864
    X473
    17592
    41048
   23456
2,773,672
```

Here's how

```
  7316
X528
```

```
  9215
X376
```

```
  6034
X129
```

```
  2364
X351
```

```
  3672
X155
```

Multiplication

Find the products.

```
   4873
  X 526
  29238
   9746
  24365
2,563,198
```

```
  6205
 X 307
```

```
  3792
 X 841
```

```
  1887
 X 645
```

```
  8546
 X 146
```

```
  2050
 X 356
```

29

Multiplication

Find the products.

7542 X1438	8963 X5742
4375 X3782	2486 X3976

©1983, Instructional Fair, In

Multiplication

Find the products.

6582	8756
X386	X555

7563	2356
X5825	X4789

Multiplicatior

Find the products.

172	56	6
X154	X485	X385

682	515	354
X121	X38	X7

4852		36
X36		X4852

©1983, Instructional Fair, I

Multiplication

Find the product.

Do the biggest problem in the world!

```
  21,367,452
X 45,782,153
```

Well done!

You have finished

Step 2

33

Division

Find the quotients.

$4\overline{)4}$ $8\overline{)24}$ $3\overline{)24}$ $9\overline{)72}$ $5\overline{)45}$

$1\overline{)7}$ $2\overline{)8}$ $7\overline{)21}$ $4\overline{)20}$ $6\overline{)30}$

$8\overline{)56}$ $5\overline{)40}$ $7\overline{)63}$ $8\overline{)64}$ $6\overline{)12}$

$9\overline{)54}$ $3\overline{)21}$ $6\overline{)36}$ $7\overline{)35}$ $2\overline{)16}$

$8\overline{)48}$ $8\overline{)32}$ $3\overline{)6}$ $9\overline{)9}$ $6\overline{)18}$

$1\overline{)5}$ $4\overline{)36}$ $8\overline{)16}$ $2\overline{)2}$ $7\overline{)14}$

$1\overline{)6}$ $6\overline{)42}$ $7\overline{)56}$ $1\overline{)3}$ $3\overline{)27}$

$1\overline{)7}$ $4\overline{)24}$ $3\overline{)15}$ $3\overline{)9}$ $4\overline{)8}$

Division

Begin Step 3

34

Division

Find the quotients.

$$\begin{array}{r} 15 \\ 5\overline{)75} \\ \underline{5} \\ 25 \\ \underline{25} \\ 0 \end{array}$$

$6\overline{)96}$ $3\overline{)57}$ $4\overline{)64}$

$4\overline{)48}$ $2\overline{)98}$ $5\overline{)70}$ $6\overline{)90}$

$7\overline{)91}$ $3\overline{)63}$ $3\overline{)84}$ $4\overline{)96}$

$6\overline{)84}$ $5\overline{)95}$ $2\overline{)24}$ $3\overline{)87}$

$4\overline{)84}$ $4\overline{)92}$ $3\overline{)81}$ $5\overline{)85}$

35

Division

Find the quotients.

Here's an example

$$8\overline{)416}$$
$$\begin{array}{r} 52 \\ 8\overline{)416} \\ 40 \\ \hline 16 \\ 16 \\ \hline 0 \end{array}$$

$$5\overline{)225} \qquad 3\overline{)147}$$

$$9\overline{)783} \qquad 6\overline{)222} \qquad 4\overline{)352}$$

$$9\overline{)234} \qquad 2\overline{)842} \qquad 7\overline{)378}$$

$$7\overline{)315} \qquad 3\overline{)291} \qquad 5\overline{)380}$$

36

Division

Find the quotients.

$$
\begin{array}{r}
841 \\
9\overline{)7569} \\
72 \\
\overline{36} \\
36 \\
\overline{09} \\
9 \\
\overline{0}
\end{array}
$$

$3\overline{)1638}$ $5\overline{)3175}$

$2\overline{)1378}$ $7\overline{)1778}$ $9\overline{)2934}$

$8\overline{)3864}$ $6\overline{)4506}$ $4\overline{)1032}$

37

Crossnumber Puzzle

Find the quotients.
Then write your answers in the cross number puzzle below.

across:

b
8)‾144‾   c
4)‾196‾   e
7)‾119‾

down:

f
6)‾2160‾   h
9)‾4158‾   a
6)‾204‾

b
9)‾153‾   d
5)‾465‾

e
8)‾848‾   g
7)‾448‾

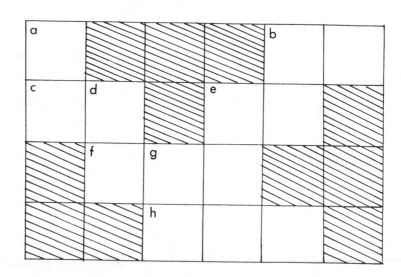

38

Crossnumber Puzzle

Find the quotients.
Then write your answers in the cross number
puzzle below.

across:

a $\quad$ e $\qquad$ f

$4\overline{)204}$ $\quad$ $6\overline{)300}$ $\quad$ $3\overline{)1260}$

down:

h $\qquad$ i $\qquad$ a

$4\overline{)364}$ $\quad$ $5\overline{)315}$ $\quad$ $9\overline{)495}$

b $\qquad$ c $\qquad$ d

$4\overline{)436}$ $\quad$ $9\overline{)396}$ $\quad$ $5\overline{)350}$

g $\qquad$ i

$7\overline{)1512}$ $\quad$ $9\overline{)135}$

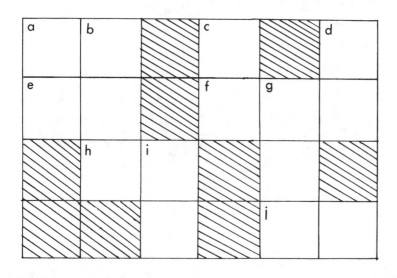

39

Division

Find the quotients.

$$\begin{array}{r} 12 \\ 14\overline{)168} \\ \underline{14} \\ 28 \\ \underline{28} \\ 0 \end{array}$$

Your example

$$33\overline{)858}\qquad 18\overline{)774}$$

$$28\overline{)672}\qquad 40\overline{)680}\qquad 43\overline{)645}$$

$$38\overline{)874}\qquad 29\overline{)928}\qquad 48\overline{)768}$$

$$16\overline{)736}\qquad 64\overline{)896}\qquad 53\overline{)583}$$

40

Division

Find the quotients.

$$14\overline{)938}$$ quotient: 67
84
98
98
0

$$83\overline{)996}$$

$$37\overline{)962}$$

$$44\overline{)792}$$

$$12\overline{)816}$$

$$21\overline{)987}$$

$$49\overline{)882}$$

$$38\overline{)722}$$

$$34\overline{)782}$$

$$46\overline{)966}$$

$$72\overline{)936}$$

$$66\overline{)990}$$

41

Division

Find the quotients.

$$24\overline{)216}$$ We did this one for you
$$\frac{9}{216}$$
$$\frac{216}{0}$$

$$52\overline{)416}$$

$$76\overline{)456}$$

$$72\overline{)432}$$

$$51\overline{)408}$$

$$30\overline{)240}$$

$$80\overline{)640}$$

$$46\overline{)322}$$

$$48\overline{)384}$$

$$96\overline{)672}$$

$$49\overline{)392}$$

$$83\overline{)747}$$

$$77\overline{)462}$$

$$18\overline{)162}$$

$$28\overline{)196}$$

42

 ©1983, Instructional Fair, I

TUTOR'S GUIDE
Mathematics Level 5

This answer section has been placed in the center of this Homework Booklet so it can be easily removed if you so desire.

The solutions in this manual reflect the layout of the exercises to simplify checking. The problem solving process as well as the solution is shown.

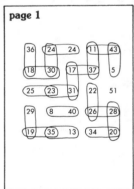

A motivational award is provided on the inside back cover. It has been designed to be signed by the tutor, either a parent or teacher.

Motivational suggestion: After the student completes each step, mark the achievement by placing a sticker next to that step shown on the award.

page 3

```
a  1958    d  789    g  47495
  +1234      -384      -47469
   3192       405        26

e  4897    i  3201    o  1687
  +3707      -1354     +1800
   8604       1847      3487

b  100     c  5555    f  347    h  24
  + 6        +3946     +340      +24
   106        9501      687       48
```

a 3	b 1	c 9	2
d 4	0	5	e 2 f 6
g 8	6	0 4	h 8
7		1 8	4 7

page 4

625	+	107	+	211	=	943
−				−		
436	+	28	+	65	=	529
−						
109	+	17	+	83	=	209
=		=		=		=
80	+	62	+	63	=	205

page 5

415	+	362	−	194	=	583
+				+		+
277	+	409	−	384	=	302
−				−		
306	+	211	−	186	=	331
=		=		=		=
386	+	560	−	392	=	554

page 6

How far from:

Willard to Springfield?	Willard to Crowley?	Spelville to Allenton?
65 km − 47 km = 18 km	65 km + 12 km = 77 km	90 km − 58 km = 32 km

Washington to Crowley?	Willard to Washington?	Crowley to Springfield?
23 km − 12 km = 11 km	65 km + 23 km = 88 km	47 km + 12 km = 59 km

page 7

Augusta to Dallas via St. Paul	Seattle to Phoenix via San Francisco	St. Louis to Tampa via New Orleans
2454 +1549 = 4003 km	1340 1296 = 2636 km	1126 1058 = 2184 km

St. Paul to New Orleans via Dallas	San Francisco to Tampa via New Orleans	Augusta to New Orleans via Cincinnati
1549 806 = 2355 km	3730 1058 = 4788 km	1622 1328 = 2950 km

page 8

Sam	Caesar	Barker	Fluffy
234 −176 = 58	218 −176 = 42	227 −176 = 51	210 −176 = 34

Corkie	Sheppie	Binky	Wagger
159 −118 = 41	147 −118 = 29	130 −118 = 12	175 −118 = 57

page 9

```
50 kg      58 kg
-42        -50
 8 kg       8 kg

           67 kg
          +20
           87 kg

           55 kg
          -47
            8 kg
```

page 10

```
 84         75 years
-11        -73
 73 years    2 years
 with the    before the
 circus      celebration

 73
x 5000
365,000 miles

 4 yards     73 years
x 3 suits   x 12 yards per
12 yards of  146     year
 fabric      73
 per year    876 yards of
              fabric
```

page 11

```
            13
           +76 years
            89 years old

 76 years    3,952 weeks
x 52 weeks   x  8 shows
 152        31,616 shows
 380
3,952 weeks

        31,616 shows
        x 100 meters
3,161,600 meters= 3,161.6 Km.
```

page 12

```
 21 lbs.
x  4
 84 lbs.

 93 lbs.
+84
177 lbs.

115 lbs.
- 97
 18 lbs.
```

page 13

x	8	4	6	9	7
9	72	36	54	81	63
6	48	24	36	54	42
7	56	28	42	63	49
8	64	32	48	72	56
5	40	20	30	45	35

page 14

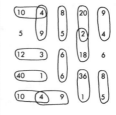

Solutions

page 15

X	9	4	8	2	6
5	45	20	40	10	30
8	72	32	64	16	48
0	0	0	0	0	0
7	63	28	56	14	42
1	9	4	8	2	6

page 16

```
a) 76    b) 7    c) 63    d) 36    e) 85
  X12      X7      X3      X18      X5
  152      49     189      288      425
   76                       36
  912                      648
```

```
f) 14    g) 8    h) 110   i) 13    j) 11
  X14      X6      X9      X14      X4
   56      48     990       52       44
   14                       13
  196                      182
```

```
9 1 2    4 9
  9      1 8 9
  6 4 8 0
    4 2 5
```

page 17

```
48    72     35     45
X2    X8     X9     X4
96   576    315    180

42    57     36     65
X3    X6     X8     X3
126  342    288    195

72    45     28     87
X9    X3     X7     X5
648  135    196    435

53    42     81     91
X4    X5     X7     X3
212  210    567    273

76    48     89     47
X5    X2     X3     X3
380   96    267    141
```

page 18

```
675     487     623
X3      X6      X4
2,025   2922    2,492

942     425     287
X6      X7      X6
5652    2975    1,722

243     496     475
X4      X2      X2
972     992     950

264     434     156
X3      X6      X7
792     2,604   1,092

272     306     344
X6      X7      X9
1,632   2,142   3,096
```

page 19

```
12            14 X 8 = 112
X             +
6  X 16 = 96
=             =
72           110 = 21 + 89
              X       X
             8   6   5
              =       =
7 X 18 = 126   445
X     =
15   144 = 8 X 18
=
105
```

page 20

```
23      46      89
X58     X98     X53
184     368     267
115     414     445
1,334   4,508   4,717

27      54      48
X46     X37     X26
162     378     288
108     162     96
1,242   1,998   1,248

93      67      68
X71     X58     X68
93      536     544
651     335     408
6,603   3,886   4,624

51      34      62
X76     X48     X89
306     272     558
357     136     496
3,876   1,632   5,518
```

page 21

```
36      452     6489
X4      X3      X9
144     1356    58,401

54      368     6751
X3      X2      X4
162     736     27,004

48      251     4381
X28     X64     X72
384     1004    8762
96      1506    30667
1,344   16,064  315,432

78      524     5483
X47     X47     X91
546     3668    5483
312     2096    49347
3,666   24,628  498,953
```

page 22

```
648     375     926
X17     X68     X84
4536    3000    3704
648     2250    7408
11,016  25,500  77,784

498     836     547
X29     X30     X49
4482    000     4923
996     2508    2188
14,442  25,080  26,803

560     213     605
X51     X42     X58
560     426     4840
2800    852     3025
28,560  8,946   35,090

743     649     711
X58     X34     X87
5944    2596    4977
3715    1947    5688
43,094  22,066  61,857
```

page 23

```
193     749     675
X76     X42     X23
1158    1498    2025
1351    2996    1350
14,668  31,458  15,525

657     238     326
X43     X54     X47
1971    952     2282
2628    1190    1304
28,251  12,852  15,322

421     317     254
X18     X29     X78
3368    2853    2032
421     634     1778
7,578   9,193   19,812

487     492     389
X56     X36     X26
2922    2952    2334
2435    1476    778
27,272  17,712  10,114
```

page 24

```
702      568
X415     X172
3510     1136
702      3976
2808     568
291,330  97,696

886      450
X359     X217
7974     3150
4430     450
2658     900
318,074  97,650

732      598
X648     X392
5856     1196
2928     5382
4392     1794
474,336  234,416
```

page 25

```
172      539
X154     X277
688      3773
860      3773
172      1078
26,488   149,303

658      427
X431     X793
658      1281
1974     3843
2632     2989
283,598  338,611

395      648
X235     X579
1975     5832
1185     4536
790      3240
92,825   375,192
```

page 26

```
5284     7334
X31      X28
5284     58672
5284     14668
15852    205,352
163,804

6920     4372
X84      X96
27680    26232
55360    39348
581,280  419,712

2432     3583
X12      X49
4864     32247
2432     14332
29,184   175,567
```

Solutions

page 27

```
 2075        6724
  X87         X16
14525       40344
16600        6724
180,525    107,584


 7926        5381
  X40         X64
 0000       21524
31704       32286
317,040    344,384


 4562        2831
  X35         X52
22810        5662
13686       14155
159,670    147,212
```

page 28

```
 5864        7316
 X473        X528
17592       58528
41048       14632
23456       36580
2,773,672  3,862,848


 9215        6034
 X376        X129
55290       54306
64505       12068
27645        6034
3,464,840   778,386


 2364        3672
 X351        X155
 2364       18360
11820       18360
 7092        3672
829,764    569,160
```

page 29

```
 4873        6205
 X526        X307
29238       43435
 9746        0000
24365       18615
2,563,198  1,904,935


 3792        1887
 X841        X645
 3792        9435
15168        7548
30336       11322
3,189,072  1,217,115


 8546        2050
 X146        X356
51276       12300
34184       10250
 8546        6150
1,247,716  729,800
```

page 30

```
  7542         8963
 X1438        X5742
 60336        17926
 22626        35852
 30168        62741
  7542        44815
10,845,396  51,465,546


  4375         2486
 X3782        X3976
  8750        14916
 35000        17402
 30625        22374
 13125         7458
16,546,250   9,884,336
```

page 31

```
 6582         8756
 X386         X555
39492        43780
52656        43780
19746        43780
2,540,652   4,859,580


 7563          2356
X5825         X4789
37815         21204
15126         18848
60504         16492
37815          9424
44,054,475  11,282,884
```

page 32

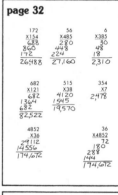

```
  172      56       6
 X154     X485     X385
  688      280      30
  860      448      48
  172      224      18
26,488   27,160   2,310


  682      515      354
 X121      X38       X7
  682     4120     2,478
 1364     1545
  682    19,570
82,522


 4852              36
  X36           X4852
29112             72
14556            180
174,672          288
                 144
               174,672
```

page 33

```
    21,367,452
  X45,782,153
     64102356
    106837260
     21367452
     42734904
    170939616
    149572164
    106837260
     85469808
978,247,956,684,156
```

page 34

```
 1        3        8        8        9
4)4     8)24     3)24     9)72     5)45

 7        4        3        5        5
1)7     2)8      7)21     4)20     6)30

 7        8        9        8        2
8)56    5)40     7)63     8)64     6)12

 6        3        6        5        8
9)54    7)21     6)36     7)35     2)16

 6        4        2        1        3
8)48    8)32     3)6      9)9      6)18

 5        9        2        1        2
1)5     4)36     8)16     2)2      7)14

 6        7        8        3        9
1)6     6)42     7)56     1)3      3)27

 7        6        5        3        2
1)7     4)24     3)15     3)9      4)8
```

page 35

```
  15       16       19       16
5)75     6)96     3)57     4)64

  12       49       14       15
4)48     2)98     5)70     6)90

         7)91    3)63     3)84

  14       19       12       24
6)84     5)95     2)24     4)96

  21       23       27       17
8)84     4)92     3)81     5)85
```

page 36

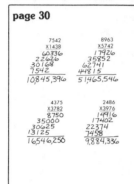

```
  52       45       49
8)416    5)225    3)147

  87       37       88
9)783    6)222    4)352

  26      421       54
9)234    2)842    7)378

  45               76
7)315    3)291    5)380
```

page 37

```
   841      546      635
9)7569   3)1638   5)3175


   689      254      326
2)1378   7)1778   9)2934


   483      751      258
8)3864   6)4506   4)1032
```

page 38

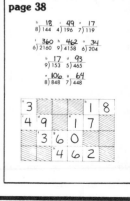

```
  b 18   c 49   e 17
8)144   4)196  7)119

  f 360  h 462  g 34
6)2160  9)4158 6)204

  h 17   d 93
9)153   5)465

  g 106  e 64
8)848   7)448
```

©1983, Instructional Fair, Inc

page 39

page 40

page 41

page 42

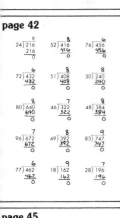

page 43

page 44

page 45

page 46

page 47

page 48

page 49

page 50

Solutions

Solutions

page 51

$\left(\frac{1}{2} = \frac{3}{6}\right)$ $\frac{1}{2} = \frac{3}{8}$ $\left(\frac{1}{4} = \frac{2}{8}\right)$

$\left(\frac{1}{3} = \frac{2}{6}\right)$ $\left(\frac{2}{4} = \frac{1}{2}\right)$ $\frac{1}{3} = \frac{1}{4}$

$\left(\frac{2}{3} = \frac{4}{6}\right)$ $\left(\frac{4}{4} = \frac{2}{2}\right)$ $\left(\frac{4}{8} = \frac{1}{2}\right)$

$\frac{1}{8} = \frac{2}{3}$ $\left(\frac{6}{8} = \frac{3}{4}\right)$ $\frac{1}{2} = \frac{7}{8}$

$\frac{1}{8} = \frac{1}{6}$ $\frac{1}{4} = \frac{3}{6}$ $\left(\frac{4}{8} = \frac{3}{6}\right)$

$\frac{1}{2} = \frac{4}{6}$ $\frac{1}{3} = \frac{3}{8}$ $\frac{1}{2} = \frac{5}{8}$

page 52

$\frac{1}{2} = \frac{2}{4}$ $\frac{1}{4} = \frac{2}{8}$ $\frac{3}{5} = \frac{6}{10}$

$\frac{4}{10} = \frac{2}{5}$ $\frac{5}{10} = \frac{1}{2}$ $\frac{4}{8} = \frac{5}{10}$

$\frac{4}{4} = \frac{10}{10}$ $\frac{4}{5} = \frac{8}{10}$ $\frac{1}{2} = \frac{5}{10}$

$\frac{1}{2} = \frac{3}{6}$ $\frac{1}{3} = \frac{2}{6}$ $\frac{3}{4} = \frac{6}{8}$

$\frac{2}{3} = \frac{4}{6}$ $\frac{1}{2} = \frac{4}{8}$ $\frac{8}{10} = \frac{4}{5}$

page 53

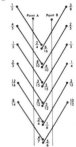

They appear to get a little closer

page 54

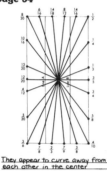

They appear to curve away from each other in the center

page 55

$\frac{5}{20} = \frac{1}{4}$ $\frac{8}{20} = \frac{2}{5}$ $\frac{3}{15} = \frac{1}{5}$

$\frac{12}{20} = \frac{3}{5}$ $\frac{2}{8} = \frac{1}{4}$ $\frac{12}{16} = \frac{3}{4}$

$\frac{14}{16} = \frac{7}{8}$ $\frac{4}{8} = \frac{1}{2}$ $\frac{9}{12} = \frac{3}{4}$

$\frac{5}{10} = \frac{1}{2}$ $\frac{6}{10} = \frac{3}{5}$ $\frac{2}{4} = \frac{1}{2}$

page 56

$\frac{4}{20} = \frac{1}{5}$ $\frac{6}{20} = \frac{3}{10}$ $\frac{8}{20} = \frac{2}{5}$

$\frac{9}{15} = \frac{3}{5}$ $\frac{4}{10} = \frac{2}{5}$ $\frac{8}{10} = \frac{4}{5}$

$\frac{2}{10} = \frac{1}{5}$ $\frac{3}{15} = \frac{1}{5}$ $\frac{6}{20} = \frac{3}{10}$

$\frac{12}{20} = \frac{3}{5}$ $\frac{10}{20} = \frac{1}{2}$ $\frac{6}{10} = \frac{3}{5}$

page 57

$\frac{3}{2} = 1\frac{1}{2}$ $\frac{7}{5} = 1\frac{2}{5}$ $\frac{9}{8} = 1\frac{1}{8}$

$\frac{11}{9} = 1\frac{2}{9}$ $\frac{4}{3} = 1\frac{1}{3}$ $\frac{13}{6} = 2\frac{1}{6}$

$1\frac{1}{4} = \frac{5}{4}$ $1\frac{1}{5} = \frac{6}{5}$ $1\frac{3}{4} = \frac{7}{4}$

$1\frac{1}{3} = \frac{4}{3}$ $1\frac{5}{6} = \frac{11}{6}$ $1\frac{4}{9} = \frac{13}{9}$

page 58

$\frac{15}{8} = 1\frac{7}{8}$ $\frac{11}{3} = 3\frac{2}{3}$ $\frac{12}{5} = 2\frac{2}{5}$

$\frac{7}{4} = 1\frac{3}{4}$ $\frac{11}{4} = 2\frac{3}{4}$ $\frac{7}{2} = 3\frac{1}{2}$

$\frac{10}{3} = 3\frac{1}{3}$ $\frac{11}{5} = 2\frac{1}{5}$ $\frac{10}{7} = 1\frac{3}{7}$

$2\frac{1}{4} = \frac{9}{4}$ $3\frac{2}{3} = \frac{11}{3}$ $1\frac{4}{6} = \frac{10}{6}$

$3\frac{1}{5} = \frac{16}{5}$ $1\frac{4}{5} = \frac{9}{5}$ $3\frac{1}{2} = \frac{7}{2}$

$4\frac{1}{3} = \frac{13}{3}$ $2\frac{1}{8} = \frac{17}{8}$ $4\frac{1}{3} = \frac{13}{3}$

page 59

$\begin{array}{r}4\frac{1}{5}\\+3\frac{2}{5}\\\hline 7\frac{3}{5}\end{array}$ $\begin{array}{r}7\frac{2}{6}\\+1\frac{1}{6}\\\hline 8\frac{3}{6}\end{array}$ $\begin{array}{r}3\frac{1}{4}\\+2\frac{1}{4}\\\hline 5\frac{2}{4}\end{array}$ $\begin{array}{r}4\frac{3}{8}\\+5\frac{5}{8}\\\hline 9\frac{8}{8}\end{array}$

$\begin{array}{r}2\frac{2}{7}\\+8\frac{5}{7}\\\hline 10\frac{7}{7}\end{array}$ $\begin{array}{r}1\frac{5}{12}\\+8\frac{7}{12}\\\hline 9\frac{12}{12}\end{array}$ $\begin{array}{r}5\frac{1}{16}\\+2\frac{4}{16}\\\hline 7\frac{5}{16}\end{array}$ $\begin{array}{r}3\frac{1}{10}\\+6\frac{6}{10}\\\hline 9\frac{7}{10}\end{array}$

$\begin{array}{r}2\frac{2}{8}\\+3\frac{3}{8}\\\hline 5\frac{5}{8}\end{array}$ $\begin{array}{r}3\frac{4}{8}\\+5\frac{4}{8}\\\hline 8\frac{8}{8}\end{array}$ $\begin{array}{r}2\frac{3}{13}\\+4\frac{5}{13}\\\hline 6\frac{8}{13}\end{array}$ $\begin{array}{r}2\frac{6}{10}\\+6\frac{4}{10}\\\hline 8\frac{10}{10}\end{array}$

$\begin{array}{r}2\frac{1}{8}\\+3\frac{4}{8}\\\hline 5\frac{5}{8}\end{array}$ $\begin{array}{r}5\frac{1}{16}\\+3\frac{9}{16}\\\hline 8\frac{10}{16}\end{array}$ $\begin{array}{r}6\frac{1}{3}\\+3\frac{1}{3}\\\hline 9\frac{2}{3}\end{array}$ $\begin{array}{r}9\frac{1}{10}\\+3\frac{9}{10}\\\hline 12\frac{10}{10}\end{array}$

page 60

$\begin{array}{r}4\frac{7}{8}\\-1\frac{4}{8}\\\hline 3\frac{3}{8}\end{array}$ $\begin{array}{r}4\frac{4}{5}\\-2\frac{2}{5}\\\hline 2\frac{2}{5}\end{array}$ $\begin{array}{r}8\frac{4}{6}\\-3\frac{1}{6}\\\hline 5\frac{3}{6}\end{array}$ $\begin{array}{r}4\frac{3}{4}\\-1\frac{1}{4}\\\hline 3\frac{2}{4}\end{array}$

$\begin{array}{r}6\frac{4}{7}\\-2\frac{3}{7}\\\hline 4\frac{1}{7}\end{array}$ $\begin{array}{r}9\frac{12}{13}\\-3\frac{4}{13}\\\hline 6\frac{8}{13}\end{array}$ $\begin{array}{r}10\frac{14}{16}\\-7\frac{10}{16}\\\hline 3\frac{4}{16}\end{array}$ $\begin{array}{r}7\frac{6}{10}\\-4\frac{4}{10}\\\hline 3\frac{2}{10}\end{array}$

$\begin{array}{r}4\frac{4}{8}\\-3\frac{3}{8}\\\hline 1\frac{1}{8}\end{array}$ $\begin{array}{r}8\frac{11}{15}\\-5\frac{5}{15}\\\hline 3\frac{6}{15}\end{array}$ $\begin{array}{r}9\frac{6}{10}\\-7\frac{4}{10}\\\hline 2\frac{2}{10}\end{array}$ $\begin{array}{r}8\frac{7}{10}\\-4\frac{4}{10}\\\hline 4\frac{3}{10}\end{array}$

$\begin{array}{r}6\frac{18}{20}\\-4\frac{10}{20}\\\hline 2\frac{8}{20}\end{array}$ $\begin{array}{r}4\frac{4}{5}\\-1\frac{1}{2}\\\hline 3\frac{1}{2}\end{array}$ $\begin{array}{r}5\frac{4}{5}\\-2\frac{1}{5}\\\hline 3\frac{3}{5}\end{array}$ $\begin{array}{r}9\frac{6}{12}\\-4\frac{4}{12}\\\hline 4\frac{2}{12}\end{array}$

page 61

$\begin{array}{r}4\frac{3}{10}\\2\frac{6}{10}\\+1\frac{1}{10}\\\hline 7\frac{10}{10}\end{array}$ $\begin{array}{r}3\frac{1}{4}\\1\frac{1}{4}\\+2\frac{1}{4}\\\hline 6\frac{3}{4}\end{array}$ $\begin{array}{r}1\frac{1}{3}\\4\frac{1}{3}\\+2\frac{1}{3}\\\hline 7\frac{3}{3}\end{array}$ $\begin{array}{r}8\frac{2}{8}\\1\frac{3}{8}\\+4\frac{3}{8}\\\hline 13\frac{8}{8}\end{array}$

$\begin{array}{r}2\frac{1}{3}\\4\frac{1}{3}\\+3\frac{1}{3}\\\hline 9\frac{3}{3}\end{array}$ $\begin{array}{r}3\frac{2}{6}\\4\frac{2}{6}\\+4\frac{2}{6}\\\hline 10\frac{6}{6}\end{array}$ $\begin{array}{r}1\frac{2}{7}\\2\frac{2}{7}\\+4\frac{3}{7}\\\hline 7\frac{7}{7}\end{array}$ $\begin{array}{r}2\frac{1}{10}\\3\frac{3}{10}\\+2\frac{3}{10}\\\hline 7\frac{7}{10}\end{array}$

$\begin{array}{r}3\frac{8}{10}\\-2\frac{2}{10}\\\hline 1\frac{6}{10}\end{array}$ $\begin{array}{r}5\frac{4}{7}\\-1\frac{3}{7}\\\hline 4\frac{1}{7}\end{array}$ $\begin{array}{r}3\frac{5}{6}\\-1\frac{4}{6}\\\hline 2\frac{1}{6}\end{array}$ $\begin{array}{r}9\frac{3}{4}\\-3\frac{1}{4}\\\hline 6\frac{2}{4}\end{array}$

$\begin{array}{r}4\frac{11}{12}\\-3\frac{5}{12}\\\hline 1\frac{6}{12}\end{array}$ $\begin{array}{r}7\frac{6}{8}\\-4\frac{3}{8}\\\hline 3\frac{3}{8}\end{array}$ $\begin{array}{r}7\frac{6}{6}\\-2\frac{4}{6}\\\hline 5\frac{2}{6}\end{array}$ $\begin{array}{r}8\frac{3}{5}\\-5\frac{2}{5}\\\hline 3\frac{1}{5}\end{array}$

page 62

$\frac{2}{4} + \frac{3}{4} = \frac{5}{4}$

$\frac{5}{4} = 1\frac{1}{4}$

$\frac{1}{3} + \frac{1}{3} + \frac{3}{3} = \frac{5}{3}$

$\frac{5}{3} = 1\frac{2}{3}$

$\frac{1}{2} + \frac{1}{2} + \frac{1}{2} = \frac{3}{2}$

$\frac{3}{2} = 1\frac{1}{2}$

$\frac{7}{8} + \frac{4}{8} = \frac{11}{8}$

$\frac{12}{8} = 1\frac{4}{8} = 1\frac{1}{2}$

$\frac{3}{8} + \frac{7}{8} = \frac{10}{8}$

$\frac{10}{8} = 1\frac{2}{8} = 1\frac{1}{4}$

$\frac{3}{5} + \frac{3}{5} = \frac{6}{5}$

$\frac{6}{5} = 1\frac{1}{5}$

page 63

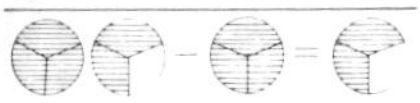

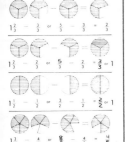

$1\frac{2}{3} - \frac{3}{3}$ or $\frac{5}{3} - \frac{3}{3} = \frac{2}{3}$

$1\frac{2}{3} - \frac{2}{3}$ or $\frac{5}{3} - \frac{2}{3} = \frac{3}{3}$ or 1

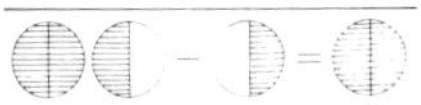

$1\frac{1}{2} - \frac{1}{2}$ or $\frac{3}{2} - \frac{1}{2} = \frac{2}{2}$ or 1

$1\frac{3}{5} - \frac{4}{5}$ or $\frac{8}{5} - \frac{4}{5} = \frac{4}{5}$

page 64

$\frac{1}{2}=\frac{3}{6}$, $+\frac{1}{3}=\frac{2}{6}$, $\frac{5}{6}$

$\frac{2}{5}=\frac{4}{10}$, $+\frac{3}{10}=\frac{3}{10}$, $\frac{7}{10}$

$\frac{1}{4}=\frac{1}{4}$, $+\frac{1}{2}=\frac{2}{4}$, $\frac{3}{4}$

$\frac{1}{8}=\frac{1}{8}$, $+\frac{1}{4}=\frac{2}{8}$, $\frac{3}{8}$

$\frac{1}{12}=\frac{1}{12}$, $+\frac{1}{3}=\frac{4}{12}$, $\frac{5}{12}$

$\frac{1}{10}=\frac{1}{10}$, $+\frac{1}{5}=\frac{2}{10}$, $\frac{3}{10}$

page 65

$\frac{1}{2}=\frac{5}{10}$, $-\frac{1}{5}=\frac{2}{10}$, $\frac{3}{10}$

$\frac{1}{3}=\frac{4}{12}$, $-\frac{1}{4}=\frac{3}{12}$, $\frac{1}{12}$

$\frac{1}{3}=\frac{2}{6}$, $-\frac{1}{6}=\frac{1}{6}$, $\frac{1}{6}$

$\frac{2}{3}=\frac{10}{15}$, $-\frac{2}{5}=\frac{6}{15}$, $\frac{4}{15}$

$\frac{5}{9}=\frac{10}{18}$, $-\frac{1}{2}=\frac{9}{18}$, $\frac{1}{18}$

$\frac{2}{3}=\frac{4}{6}$, $-\frac{1}{2}=\frac{3}{6}$, $\frac{1}{6}$

page 66

$\frac{5}{6}=\frac{5}{6}$, $-\frac{2}{3}=\frac{4}{6}$, $\frac{1}{6}$

$\frac{5}{6}=\frac{25}{30}$, $-\frac{1}{5}=\frac{6}{30}$, $\frac{19}{30}$

$\frac{2}{3}=\frac{8}{12}$, $+\frac{1}{4}=\frac{3}{12}$, $\frac{11}{12}$

$\frac{3}{4}=\frac{9}{12}$, $-\frac{1}{3}=\frac{4}{12}$, $\frac{5}{12}$

$\frac{5}{12}=\frac{5}{12}$, $+\frac{1}{6}=\frac{2}{12}$, $\frac{7}{12}$

$\frac{4}{5}=\frac{8}{10}$, $-\frac{5}{10}=\frac{5}{10}$, $\frac{3}{10}$

$\frac{5}{12}=\frac{5}{12}$, $-\frac{1}{3}=\frac{4}{12}$, $\frac{1}{12}$

$\frac{9}{12}=\frac{9}{12}$, $+\frac{1}{6}=\frac{2}{12}$, $\frac{11}{12}$

$\frac{1}{3}=\frac{5}{15}$, $+\frac{1}{5}=\frac{3}{15}$, $\frac{8}{15}$

$\frac{1}{3}=\frac{3}{9}$, $+\frac{2}{9}=\frac{2}{9}$, $\frac{5}{9}$

$\frac{3}{4}=\frac{15}{20}$, $-\frac{2}{5}=\frac{8}{20}$, $\frac{7}{20}$

$\frac{3}{5}=\frac{6}{10}$, $+\frac{1}{10}=\frac{1}{10}$, $\frac{7}{10}$

page 67

$\frac{11}{12}=\frac{11}{12}$, $-\frac{1}{4}=\frac{3}{12}$, $\frac{8}{12}=\frac{2}{3}$

$\frac{2}{3}=\frac{4}{6}$, $-\frac{1}{6}=\frac{1}{6}$, $\frac{3}{6}=\frac{1}{2}$

$\frac{13}{15}=\frac{13}{15}$, $-\frac{2}{3}=\frac{10}{15}$, $\frac{3}{15}=\frac{1}{5}$

$\frac{11}{14}=\frac{11}{14}$, $-\frac{1}{2}=\frac{7}{14}$, $\frac{4}{14}=\frac{2}{7}$

$\frac{7}{12}=\frac{7}{12}$, $-\frac{1}{4}=\frac{3}{12}$, $\frac{4}{12}=\frac{1}{3}$

$\frac{11}{18}=\frac{11}{18}$, $-\frac{1}{2}=\frac{9}{18}$, $\frac{2}{18}=\frac{1}{9}$

page 68

$\frac{2}{3}=\frac{8}{12}$, $+\frac{3}{4}=\frac{9}{12}$, $\frac{17}{12}=1\frac{5}{12}$

$\frac{5}{7}=\frac{10}{14}$, $+\frac{1}{2}=\frac{7}{14}$, $\frac{17}{14}=1\frac{3}{14}$

$\frac{5}{8}=\frac{5}{8}$, $+\frac{3}{4}=\frac{6}{8}$, $\frac{11}{8}=1\frac{3}{8}$

$\frac{1}{3}=\frac{4}{12}$, $+\frac{3}{4}=\frac{9}{12}$, $\frac{13}{12}=1\frac{1}{12}$

$\frac{4}{5}=\frac{12}{15}$, $+\frac{2}{3}=\frac{10}{15}$, $\frac{22}{15}=1\frac{7}{15}$

$\frac{1}{2}=\frac{3}{6}$, $+\frac{2}{3}=\frac{4}{6}$, $\frac{7}{6}=1\frac{1}{6}$

page 69

$\frac{5}{8}=\frac{13}{8}$, $-\frac{7}{8}=\frac{7}{8}$, $\frac{6}{8}=\frac{3}{4}$

$1\frac{1}{9}=\frac{10}{9}$, $-\frac{7}{9}=\frac{7}{9}$, $\frac{3}{9}=\frac{1}{3}$

$1\frac{1}{7}=\frac{8}{7}$, $-\frac{6}{7}=\frac{6}{7}$, $\frac{2}{7}$

$1\frac{1}{12}=\frac{13}{12}$, $-\frac{5}{12}=\frac{5}{12}$, $\frac{8}{12}=\frac{2}{3}$

$1\frac{3}{5}=\frac{8}{5}$, $-\frac{4}{5}=\frac{4}{5}$, $\frac{4}{5}$

$1\frac{1}{6}=\frac{7}{6}$, $-\frac{5}{6}=\frac{5}{6}$, $\frac{2}{6}=\frac{1}{3}$

page 70

$1\frac{1}{12}=\frac{13}{12}$, $-\frac{1}{3}=\frac{4}{12}$, $\frac{9}{12}=\frac{3}{4}$

$1\frac{1}{8}=\frac{9}{8}$, $-\frac{1}{2}=\frac{4}{8}$, $\frac{5}{8}$

$1\frac{1}{8}=\frac{9}{8}$, $-\frac{3}{4}=\frac{6}{8}$, $\frac{3}{8}$

$1\frac{5}{8}=\frac{13}{8}$, $-\frac{3}{4}=\frac{6}{8}$, $\frac{7}{8}$

$1\frac{5}{6}=\frac{11}{6}$, $-\frac{2}{3}=\frac{4}{6}$, $\frac{7}{6}=1\frac{1}{6}$

$1\frac{1}{10}=\frac{11}{10}$, $-\frac{1}{2}=\frac{5}{10}$, $\frac{6}{10}=\frac{3}{5}$

page 71

Name \ height	last year	this year	growth
Don	5'8½"	5' 9⅛"	$\frac{5}{8}$"
Barbara	5'⅜"	5'1¼"	$\frac{7}{8}$"
Janice	4'10¾"	4'11⅜"	$\frac{5}{8}$"
Murray	4'6⅞"	4'7½"	$\frac{5}{8}$"
Lois	4'2"	4'5½"	$3\frac{1}{2}$"
Kara	3'10½"	3'11¾"	$1\frac{1}{4}$"

Don: $9\frac{1}{8}" = 8\frac{9}{8}"$, $-8\frac{1}{2} = 8\frac{4}{8}$, $\frac{5}{8}"$

Barbara: $1\frac{1}{4}" = \frac{10}{8}"$, $-\frac{3}{8} = \frac{3}{8}$, $\frac{7}{8}"$

Janice: $11\frac{3}{8}" = 10\frac{11}{8}"$, $-10\frac{3}{4} = 10\frac{6}{8}$, $\frac{5}{8}"$

Murray: $7\frac{1}{2}" = 6\frac{12}{8}"$, $-6\frac{7}{8} = 6\frac{7}{8}$, $\frac{5}{8}"$

Lois: $5\frac{1}{2}"$, -2, $3\frac{1}{2}"$

Kara: $11\frac{3}{4}" = 11\frac{3}{4}"$, $-10\frac{1}{2} = 10\frac{2}{4}$, $1\frac{1}{4}$

page 72

3.6 + 3.3 = 6.9	4.2 + 5.2 = 9.4	6.4 + 1.4 = 7.8	3.1 + 7.8 = 10.9
4.7 + 3.2 = 7.9	4.9 + 2.0 = 6.9	3.4 + 1.2 = 4.6	8.2 + 1.6 = 9.8
6.8 − 2.6 = 4.2	5.9 − 3.2 = 2.7	6.7 − 5.6 = 1.1	7.8 − 2.5 = 5.3
5.8 − 3.3 = 2.5	3.9 − 1.5 = 2.4	5.8 − 2.2 = 3.6	4.7 − 3.4 = 1.3
3.4 + 5.3 = 8.7	6.6 + 1.2 = 7.8	4.7 − 2.3 = 2.4	3.9 − 2.7 = 1.2

page 73

.97 − .44 = .53	.74 − .43 = .31	.35 + .44 = .79	.16 + .22 = .38

6.73 + 1.15 = 7.88	4.27 + 5.52 = 9.79	3.46 + 2.31 = 5.77
6.37 + 3.52 = 9.89	5.47 + 1.32 = 6.79	4.53 + 2.41 = 6.94
9.97 − 3.32 = 6.65	7.65 − 4.21 = 3.44	2.98 − 1.63 = 1.35
5.97 − 2.84 = 3.13	9.87 − 3.75 = 6.12	6.97 − 4.76 = 2.21

page 74

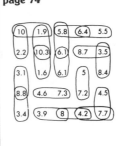

10	1.9	5.8	6.4	5.5
2.2	10.3	6.1	8.7	3.5
3.1	1.6	6.1	5	8.4
8.8	4.6	7.3	7.2	4.5
3.4	3.9	8	4.2	7.7

Solutions

page 75

¹.236 +.821 1.057	¹.323 +.845 1.168	¹.546 +.853 1.399
4.964 +3.753 8.717	4.652 +2.747 7.399	3.864 +1.117 4.981
.954 −.763 .191	.652 −.581 .071	.864 −.173 .691
2.796 −1.385 1.411	9.938 −6.948 2.990	5.786 −3.493 2.293
5.879 −3.785 2.094	8.879 −2.892 5.987	6.854 +2.921 9.775

page 76

3.25 5.73 +4.21 13.19	3.82 4.15 +2.38 10.35	4.73 2.49 +5.82 13.04
8.263 −3.352 4.911	9.305 −6.283 3.022	9.200 −3.032 6.168
9.975 −7.871 2.104	6.895 −4.174 2.721	1.589 −.306 1.283
3.441 6.567 +3.128 13.136	4.214 2.389 +6.463 13.066	3.564 6.038 +2.719 12.321

page 77

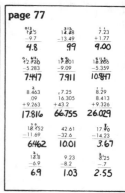

12.5 −9.7 = 4.8	12.48 −13.49 = .99	7.23 +1.77 = 9.00
12.730 −5.283 = 7.447	15.801 −9.09 = 7.911	12.206 −5.359 = 10.847
8.463 / .09 / +9.263 = 17.816	7.25 / 16.305 / +43.2 = 66.755	8.29 / 8.413 / +9.326 = 26.029
18.152 −11.69 = 6.462	42.61 −32.6 = 10.01	17.90 −14.23 = 3.67
13.8 −6.9 = 6.9	9.23 −8.2 = 1.03	3.25 −.7 = 2.55

page 78

+	.3	.07	5	30	.4
9	9.3	9.07	14	39	9.4
.1	.4	.17	5.1	30.1	.5
20	20.3	20.07	25	50	20.4
.06	.36	.13	5.06	30.06	.46
.8	1.1	.87	5.8	30.8	1.2

page 79

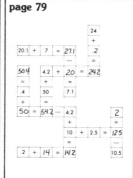

page 80

28.2 −13.8 = 12.4	3.475 +12.5 = 15.975	8.33 −.43 = 8.90
9.33 / 6.231 / +8.9 = 24.461	3.8 / 2.5 / +23.7 = 30.0	14.865 / 24.8 / +1.1 = 40.765
12.206 −7.893 = 8.307	6.005 +3.499 = 9.504	4.182 −3.295 = .887
15.01 / .002 / 6.16 / +35.213 = 56.385	3.152 / .02 / 26.305 / +14.003 = 43.480	4.27 / 1.002 / .219 / +27.106 = 32.597

page 81

page 82

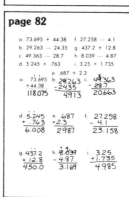

a. 73.695 + 44.38
b. 29.263 − 24.35
c. 49.363 − 28.7
d. 5.245 + .763
e. .687 + 2.3
f. 27.258 − 4.1
g. 437.2 + 12.8
h. 8.039 − 4.87
i. 3.25 + 1.735

a. 73.695 +44.38 = 118.075
b. 29.263 −24.35 = 4.913
c. 49.363 −28.7 = 20.663
d. 5.245 +.763 = 6.008
e. .687 +2.3 = 2.987
f. 27.258 −4.1 = 23.158
g. 437.2 +12.8 = 450.0
h. 8.039 −4.87 = 3.169
i. 3.25 +1.735 = 4.985

page 83

a. 9.038 + .003 + 7.305 + .35
b. 9.31 + 15.305 + 27.25 + 1.3
c. 3.25 + 1.730 + 8.3 + 42.1
d. 3.254 − .123
e. 14.465 − .234
f. 14.589 − 1.3067
g. 1.76 − .157
h. 4.97 + .435
i. 425.1 + .58

a. 9.038 +.003 +7.305 +.35 = 16.696
b. 9.31 +15.305 +27.25 +1.3 = 53.165
c. 3.25 +1.730 +8.3 +42.1 = 55.380
d. 3.254 −.123 = 3.131
e. 14.465 −.234 = 14.231
f. 14.5890 −1.3067 = 13.2823
g. 1.760 −.157 = 1.603
h. 4.97 +.435 = 5.405
i. 425.1 +.58 = 425.68

page 84

a. 14.036 − 4.341
b. 13.066 − 4.214
c. 12.321 − 2.7
d. 13.19 − 5.734
e. 10.35 − 2.3844
f. 13.04 − 1.001
g. 4.216 + .392 + 27.305 + 3.293
h. 13.26 + 2.905 + 9.7 + 46.258
i. 1.01 + .707 + 18.25 + 16.307

a. 14.036 −4.341 = 9.695
b. 13.066 −4.214 = 8.852
c. 12.321 −2.7 = 9.621
d. 13.190 −5.734 = 7.456
e. 10.3500 −2.3844 = 7.9656
f. 13.040 −1.001 = 12.039
g. 4.216 / .392 / 27.305 / +3.293 = 35.206
h. 13.26 / 2.905 / 9.7 / +46.258 = 72.123
i. 1.01 / .707 / 18.25 / +16.307 = 36.274

page 85

			$1.50	
			55	
			+.85	
			$2.90	
			$3.00	
			1.65	
			+1.70	
			$6.35	
$1.50	$.55	$.85		
+1.50	+.55	+.85		
$3.00	$1.65	$1.70		
			$4.50	
			2.20	
			+2.55	
			$9.25	
$3.00	$1.65	$1.70		
+1.50	+.55	+.85		
$4.50	$2.20	$2.55		

page 86

			$3.50
			.45
			+.50
			$4.45
		$.45	$7.00
			1.35
			+1.00
			$9.35
$3.50	.45	$.50	
+3.50	+.45	+.50	
$7.00	$1.35	$1.00	
			$10.50
			2.25
		$1.35	+1.50
			$14.25
$7.00	.45	$1.00	
+3.50	+.45	+.50	
$10.50	$2.25	$1.50	

Division

Find the quotients.

$$\begin{array}{r} 7 \\ 27\overline{)189} \\ 189 \\ \hline 0 \end{array}$$

$65\overline{)520}$

$33\overline{)231}$

$42\overline{)378}$

$73\overline{)292}$

$53\overline{)318}$

$81\overline{)243}$

$25\overline{)225}$

$90\overline{)270}$

$85\overline{)510}$

$68\overline{)272}$

$41\overline{)287}$

$38\overline{)304}$

$56\overline{)224}$

$74\overline{)222}$

Division

Find the quotients.

Here's how

```
        127
    42) 5334
        42
        113
         84
        294
        294
          0
```

26) 7644

18) 7614

47) 5358

18) 6156

41) 6232

The Homework Booklet

Division

Find the quotients.

```
      183
37) 6771        54) 6804
    37
    307
    296
    111
    111
      0
```

```
32) 9088        28) 8904
```

```
40) 9400        65) 9620
```

Division

Find the quotients.

$$82\overline{)7790}$$ $$56\overline{)7952}$$

$$37\overline{)4477}$$ $$89\overline{)4895}$$

$$44\overline{)4268}$$ $$36\overline{)5436}$$

Division

Find the quotients.

```
      48
53) 2544
    212
    424
    424
      0
```

78) 3432

36) 3456   92) 7912

57) 5586   74) 6438

84) 5796   62) 5208

47

Division

Find the quotients.

an example

```
        541
  72) 38952
      360
      295
      288
       72
       72
        0
```

43) 28939

57) 20406

44) 38412

42) 28182

79) 75208

The Homework Booklet ©1983, Instructional Fair

Division

Find the quotients.

$$8 \overline{)176}$$ $$15 \overline{)405}$$

$$45 \overline{)28260}$$ $$8 \overline{)3648}$$

$$65 \overline{)8125}$$ $$78 \overline{)3276}$$

Division

Find the quotients.

$$5\overline{)445} \qquad\qquad 35\overline{)525}$$

$$36\overline{)28404} \qquad\qquad 65\overline{)3770}$$

That's great

You have finished

Step 3

$$38\overline{)8056} \qquad\qquad 9\overline{)71037}$$

The Homework Booklet

Equivalent Fractions

Circle the pairs of equivalent fractions.

$\dfrac{1}{2} = \dfrac{3}{6}$ $\dfrac{1}{2} = \dfrac{3}{8}$ $\dfrac{1}{4} = \dfrac{2}{8}$

$\dfrac{1}{3} = \dfrac{2}{6}$ $\dfrac{2}{4} = \dfrac{1}{2}$ $\dfrac{1}{3} = \dfrac{1}{4}$

$\dfrac{2}{3} = \dfrac{4}{6}$ $\dfrac{4}{4} = \dfrac{2}{2}$ $\dfrac{4}{8} = \dfrac{1}{2}$

$\dfrac{1}{8} = \dfrac{2}{3}$ $\dfrac{6}{8} = \dfrac{3}{4}$ $\dfrac{1}{2} = \dfrac{7}{8}$

$\dfrac{1}{8} = \dfrac{1}{6}$ $\dfrac{1}{4} = \dfrac{1}{6}$ $\dfrac{4}{8} = \dfrac{3}{6}$

$\dfrac{1}{2} = \dfrac{4}{6}$ $\dfrac{1}{3} = \dfrac{3}{8}$ $\dfrac{1}{2} = \dfrac{5}{8}$

equivalent fractions: fractions that represent the same amount.

Begin Step 4 Fractions

51

Equivalent Fractions

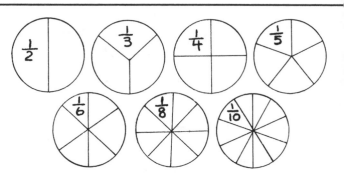

Complete each pair of equivalent fractions.

How to start

$$\boxed{\dfrac{1}{2} = \dfrac{2}{4}} \qquad \dfrac{1}{4} = \dfrac{}{8} \qquad \dfrac{3}{5} = \dfrac{}{10}$$

$$\dfrac{4}{10} = \dfrac{}{5} \qquad \dfrac{5}{10} = \dfrac{}{2} \qquad \dfrac{4}{8} = \dfrac{}{10}$$

$$\dfrac{4}{4} = \dfrac{}{10} \qquad \dfrac{4}{5} = \dfrac{}{10} \qquad \dfrac{1}{2} = \dfrac{}{10}$$

$$\dfrac{1}{2} = \dfrac{}{6} \qquad \dfrac{1}{3} = \dfrac{}{6} \qquad \dfrac{3}{4} = \dfrac{}{8}$$

$$\dfrac{2}{3} = \dfrac{}{6} \qquad \dfrac{1}{2} = \dfrac{}{8} \qquad \dfrac{8}{10} = \dfrac{}{5}$$

52

Equivalent Fractions

Match the pairs of equivalent fractions.

$\frac{1}{2}$ •   • $\frac{3}{8}$

Point A   Point B

$\frac{4}{5}$ •   • $\frac{2}{5}$

$\frac{1}{5}$ • $\frac{2}{4}$ •   • $\frac{1}{3}$
                                $\frac{6}{16}$

$\frac{2}{3}$ • $\frac{8}{10}$ •   • $\frac{1}{4}$
                                $\frac{4}{10}$

$\frac{12}{16}$ • $\frac{3}{15}$ •   • $\frac{2}{12}$
                                $\frac{5}{15}$

$\frac{8}{14}$ • $\frac{8}{12}$ •   • $\frac{10}{12}$
                                $\frac{3}{12}$

                                $\frac{3}{4}$ •
                                $\frac{1}{6}$

                                $\frac{4}{7}$ •
                                $\frac{5}{6}$

What appears to happen to "point A" and
"point B."

53

Equivalent Fractions

Match the pairs of equivalent fractions.

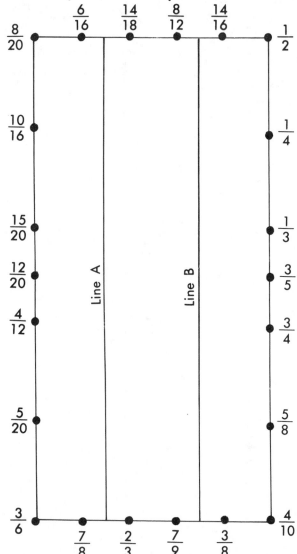

What happens to "line A" and "line B"?

The Homework Booklet

Reducing Fractions

To reduce a fraction to its lowest terms, divide both the numerator and the denominator by the largest number that will divide evenly into both.

Study this first

$$\frac{6}{20} \quad \left| \begin{array}{c} \text{think} \\ \frac{6 \div 2}{20 \div 2} \end{array} \right| = \frac{3}{10} \qquad \frac{6}{20} = \frac{3}{10}$$

Reduce each fraction to its lowest terms.

$$\frac{5}{20} = \frac{1}{4} \qquad \frac{8}{20} = \text{—} \qquad \frac{3}{15} = \text{—}$$

$$\frac{12}{20} = \text{—} \qquad \frac{2}{8} = \text{—} \qquad \frac{12}{16} = \text{—}$$

$$\frac{14}{16} = \text{—} \qquad \frac{4}{8} = \text{—} \qquad \frac{9}{12} = \text{—}$$

$$\frac{5}{10} = \text{—} \qquad \frac{6}{10} = \text{—} \qquad \frac{2}{4} = \text{—}$$

55

Reducing Fractions

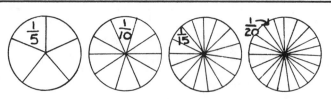

Reduce each fraction to its lowest terms.

Here's an example

$$\boxed{\frac{4}{20} = \frac{1}{5}}$$

$$\frac{6}{20} = \text{—}$$

$$\frac{8}{20} = \text{—}$$

$$\frac{9}{15} = \text{—}$$

$$\frac{4}{10} = \text{—}$$

$$\frac{8}{10} = \text{—}$$

$$\frac{2}{10} = \text{—}$$

$$\frac{3}{15} = \text{—}$$

$$\frac{6}{20} = \text{—}$$

$$\frac{12}{20} = \text{—}$$

$$\frac{10}{20} = \text{—}$$

$$\frac{6}{10} = \text{—}$$

lowest terms: when the only number that can b divided into **both** the numerator and denominato is 1.

56

Mixed Numbers

improper fraction: a fraction whose numerator is greater than its denominator; a fraction greater than 1.

$$\frac{5}{4} = \bigoplus \square = 1\frac{1}{4}$$

mixed numeral: a numeral made up of a whole number and a fraction.

Read this first

Change the improper fractions to mixed numerals.

$$\frac{3}{2} = 1\frac{1}{2} \qquad \frac{7}{5} = \underline{\quad} \qquad \frac{9}{8} = \underline{\quad}$$

$$\frac{11}{9} = \underline{\quad} \qquad \frac{4}{3} = \underline{\quad} \qquad \frac{13}{6} = \underline{\quad}$$

Change the mixed numerals to improper fractions.

$$1\frac{1}{4} = \frac{5}{4} \qquad 1\frac{1}{5} = \underline{\quad} \qquad 1\frac{3}{4} = \underline{\quad}$$

$$1\frac{1}{3} = \underline{\quad} \qquad 1\frac{5}{6} = \underline{\quad} \qquad 1\frac{4}{9} = \underline{\quad}$$

57

 ©1983, Instructional Fair, Inc.

Mixed Numbers

Change the improper fractions to mixed numerals.

$$\boxed{\frac{15}{8} = 1\frac{7}{8}} \quad \frac{11}{3} = \underline{} \quad \frac{12}{5} = \underline{}$$

$$\frac{7}{4} = \underline{} \quad \frac{11}{4} = \underline{} \quad \frac{7}{2} = \underline{}$$

$$\frac{10}{3} = \underline{} \quad \frac{11}{5} = \underline{} \quad \frac{10}{7} = \underline{}$$

Change the mixed numerals to improper fractions.

$$\boxed{2\frac{1}{4} = \frac{9}{4}} \quad 3\frac{2}{3} = \underline{} \quad 1\frac{4}{6} = \underline{}$$

$$3\frac{1}{5} = \underline{} \quad 1\frac{4}{5} = \underline{} \quad 3\frac{1}{2} = \underline{}$$

$$4\frac{1}{3} = \underline{} \quad 2\frac{1}{8} = \underline{} \quad 4\frac{1}{3} = \underline{}$$

58

Adding Mixed Numbers

Find the sums.

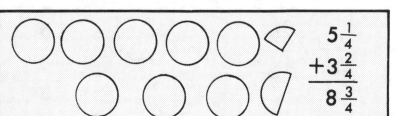

$$5\frac{1}{4}$$
$$+3\frac{2}{4}$$
$$8\frac{3}{4}$$

Here's how

$$4\frac{1}{5}$$
$$+3\frac{2}{5}$$

$$7\frac{2}{6}$$
$$+1\frac{1}{6}$$

$$3\frac{1}{4}$$
$$+2\frac{1}{4}$$

$$4\frac{5}{8}$$
$$+5\frac{1}{8}$$

$$2\frac{2}{7}$$
$$+8\frac{4}{7}$$

$$1\frac{4}{12}$$
$$+8\frac{1}{12}$$

$$5\frac{1}{16}$$
$$+2\frac{4}{16}$$

$$3\frac{3}{10}$$
$$+6\frac{4}{10}$$

$$2\frac{2}{8}$$
$$+3\frac{5}{8}$$

$$3\frac{5}{8}$$
$$+5\frac{2}{8}$$

$$2\frac{3}{15}$$
$$+4\frac{7}{15}$$

$$2\frac{2}{10}$$
$$+6\frac{4}{10}$$

$$2\frac{2}{8}$$
$$+3\frac{4}{8}$$

$$5\frac{4}{16}$$
$$+3\frac{2}{16}$$

$$6\frac{1}{3}$$
$$+3\frac{1}{3}$$

$$9\frac{7}{10}$$
$$+3\frac{1}{10}$$

59

Subtracting Mixed Numbers

Find the differences.

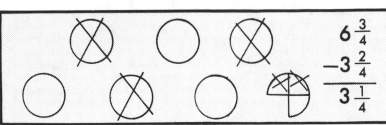

Your example

$$6\frac{3}{4}$$
$$-3\frac{2}{4}$$
$$\overline{3\frac{1}{4}}$$

$4\frac{7}{8}$	$4\frac{4}{5}$	$8\frac{5}{6}$	$4\frac{3}{4}$
$-1\frac{2}{8}$	$-2\frac{2}{5}$	$-3\frac{1}{6}$	$-1\frac{1}{4}$

$6\frac{5}{7}$	$9\frac{10}{12}$	$10\frac{15}{16}$	$7\frac{9}{10}$
$-2\frac{1}{7}$	$-3\frac{5}{12}$	$-7\frac{10}{16}$	$-4\frac{5}{10}$

$4\frac{6}{8}$	$8\frac{14}{15}$	$9\frac{9}{10}$	$8\frac{7}{10}$
$-3\frac{5}{8}$	$-5\frac{8}{15}$	$-7\frac{7}{10}$	$-4\frac{6}{10}$

$6\frac{19}{20}$	$4\frac{2}{2}$	$5\frac{3}{3}$	$9\frac{6}{12}$
$-4\frac{10}{20}$	$-1\frac{1}{2}$	$-2\frac{1}{3}$	$-5\frac{4}{12}$

60

Adding and Subtracting Mixed Numbers

Find the sums and differences.

$4\frac{3}{10}$ $3\frac{1}{4}$ $1\frac{1}{3}$ $8\frac{3}{8}$

$2\frac{4}{10}$ $1\frac{1}{4}$ $4\frac{1}{3}$ $1\frac{2}{8}$

$+1\frac{1}{10}$ $+2\frac{1}{4}$ $+2\frac{1}{3}$ $+4\frac{2}{8}$

$2\frac{3}{5}$ $3\frac{2}{6}$ $1\frac{1}{7}$ $2\frac{1}{10}$

$4\frac{1}{5}$ $3\frac{1}{6}$ $2\frac{4}{7}$ $3\frac{4}{10}$

$+3\frac{1}{5}$ $+4\frac{2}{6}$ $+4\frac{2}{7}$ $+2\frac{3}{10}$

$3\frac{8}{10}$ $5\frac{4}{7}$ $3\frac{5}{6}$ $9\frac{3}{4}$

$-2\frac{3}{10}$ $-1\frac{3}{7}$ $-1\frac{4}{6}$ $-3\frac{1}{4}$

$4\frac{11}{12}$ $7\frac{5}{8}$ $7\frac{5}{6}$ $8\frac{3}{5}$

$-3\frac{8}{12}$ $-4\frac{4}{8}$ $-2\frac{3}{6}$ $-5\frac{2}{5}$

61

Adding Fractions

Find the sums.

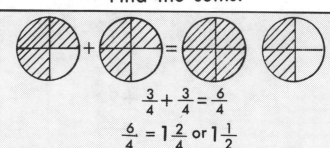

$$\frac{3}{4} + \frac{3}{4} = \frac{6}{4}$$

$$\frac{6}{4} = 1\frac{2}{4} \text{ or } 1\frac{1}{2}$$

$$\frac{2}{4} + \frac{3}{4} = \underline{\quad}$$

$$\underline{\quad} =$$

$$\frac{1}{3} + \frac{2}{3} + \frac{2}{3} = \underline{\quad}$$

$$\underline{\quad} =$$

$$\frac{1}{2} + \frac{1}{2} + \frac{1}{2} = \underline{\quad}$$

$$\underline{\quad} =$$

$$\frac{7}{8} + \frac{5}{8} = \underline{\quad}$$

$$\underline{\quad} = \quad \text{or } 1\frac{1}{2}$$

$$\frac{3}{8} + \frac{7}{8} = \underline{\quad}$$

$$\underline{\quad} = \quad \text{or } 1\frac{1}{4}$$

$$\frac{3}{5} + \frac{3}{5} = \underline{\quad}$$

$$\underline{\quad} =$$

62

Subtracting Fractions

Find the differences.

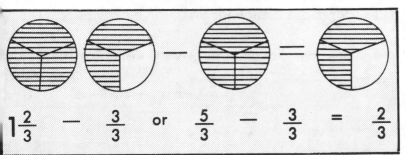

$$1\frac{2}{3} \quad - \quad \frac{3}{3} \quad \text{or} \quad \frac{5}{3} \quad - \quad \frac{3}{3} \quad = \quad \frac{2}{3}$$

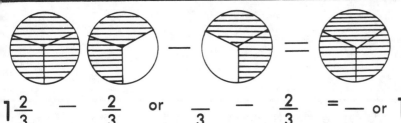

$$1\frac{2}{3} \quad - \quad \frac{2}{3} \quad \text{or} \quad \frac{\_}{3} \quad - \quad \frac{2}{3} \quad = \quad \_ \quad \text{or} \quad 1$$

$$1\frac{1}{2} \quad - \quad \frac{1}{2} \quad \text{or} \quad \frac{3}{2} \quad - \quad \frac{1}{2} \quad = \quad \_ \quad \text{or} \quad 1$$

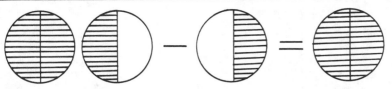

$$1\frac{3}{5} \quad - \quad \frac{4}{5} \quad \text{or} \quad \_ \quad - \quad \frac{4}{5} \quad = \quad \_$$

63

Adding Fraction:

least common denominator: lowest number into which two or more denominators can be divided.

The common denominator for these fractions is 12.

common terms: when a fractions in a problem have the same denominator.

$$\frac{1}{6}$$
$$\frac{1}{4}$$
$$\frac{1}{12}$$

$$\frac{1}{6} = \frac{2}{12}$$
$$\frac{1}{4} = \frac{3}{12}$$
$$\frac{1}{12} = \frac{1}{12}$$

Change the fractions in each problem to common terms and add.

$$\frac{1}{2} = \frac{3}{6}$$
$$+\frac{1}{3} = \frac{2}{6}$$
$$\frac{5}{6}$$

$$\frac{2}{5} =$$
$$+\frac{3}{10} =$$

$$\frac{1}{4} =$$
$$+\frac{1}{2} =$$

$$\frac{1}{8} =$$
$$+\frac{1}{4} =$$

$$\frac{1}{12} =$$
$$+\frac{1}{3} =$$

$$\frac{1}{10} =$$
$$+\frac{1}{5} =$$

Subtracting Fractions

Least common denominator: lowest number into which two or more denominators can be divided.

The common denominator for these fractions is 16.

$$\frac{1}{2}$$
$$\frac{1}{8}$$
$$\frac{1}{16}$$

common terms: when all fractions in a problem have the same denominator.

$$\frac{1}{2} = \frac{8}{16}$$
$$\frac{1}{8} = \frac{2}{16}$$
$$\frac{1}{16} = \frac{1}{16}$$

Change the fractions in each problem to common terms and subtract.

$$\frac{1}{2} = \frac{5}{10}$$
$$-\frac{1}{5} = \frac{2}{10}$$
$$\frac{3}{10}$$

$$\frac{1}{3} =$$
$$-\frac{1}{4} =$$

$$\frac{1}{3} =$$
$$-\frac{1}{6} =$$

$$\frac{2}{3} =$$
$$-\frac{2}{5} =$$

$$\frac{5}{9} =$$
$$-\frac{1}{2} =$$

$$\frac{2}{3} =$$
$$-\frac{1}{2} =$$

65

Adding an
Subtracting Fraction

Change the fractions in each problem to comm
terms and add or subtract.

We did this one for you

$$\frac{5}{6} = \frac{5}{6}$$
$$-\frac{2}{3} = \frac{4}{6}$$
$$\frac{1}{6}$$

$$\frac{5}{6} =$$
$$-\frac{1}{5} =$$

$$\frac{2}{3} =$$
$$+\frac{1}{4} =$$

$$\frac{3}{4} =$$
$$-\frac{1}{3} =$$

$$\frac{5}{12} =$$
$$+\frac{1}{6} =$$

$$\frac{4}{5} =$$
$$-\frac{5}{10} =$$

$$\frac{5}{12} =$$
$$-\frac{1}{3} =$$

$$\frac{9}{12} =$$
$$+\frac{1}{6} =$$

$$\frac{1}{3} =$$
$$+\frac{1}{5} =$$

$$\frac{1}{3} =$$
$$+\frac{2}{9} =$$

$$\frac{3}{4} =$$
$$-\frac{2}{5} =$$

$$\frac{3}{5} =$$
$$+\frac{1}{10} =$$

66

Subtracting Fractions

Change the fractions to common terms and subtract.
Reduce your answers to lowest terms if necessary.

$$\frac{11}{12} = \frac{11}{12}$$
$$-\ \frac{1}{4} = \frac{3}{12}$$
$$\frac{8}{12} = \frac{2}{3}$$

$$\frac{2}{3} =$$
$$-\ \frac{1}{6} =$$

$$\frac{13}{15} =$$
$$-\ \frac{2}{3} =$$

$$\frac{11}{14} =$$
$$-\ \frac{1}{2} =$$

$$\frac{7}{12} =$$
$$-\ \frac{1}{4} =$$

$$\frac{11}{18} =$$
$$-\ \frac{1}{2} =$$

67

Adding Fraction◌

Change the fractions to common terms and a◌
Change your answers to a mixed number if necessar◌

Here's an example

$$\frac{2}{3} = \frac{8}{12}$$
$$+\frac{3}{4} = \frac{9}{12}$$
$$\overline{\frac{17}{12} = 1\frac{5}{12}}$$

$$\frac{5}{7} =$$
$$+\frac{1}{2} =$$

$$\frac{5}{8} =$$
$$+\frac{3}{4} =$$

$$\frac{1}{3} =$$
$$+\frac{3}{4} =$$

$$\frac{4}{5} =$$
$$+\frac{2}{3} =$$

$$\frac{1}{2} =$$
$$+\frac{2}{3} =$$

ubtracting Fractions

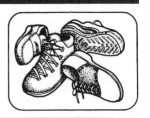

Change the mixed numeral in each problem to an improper fraction and subtract. Reduce your answers to lowest terms if necessary.

$$\frac{5}{8} = \frac{13}{8}$$
$$-\frac{7}{8} = \frac{7}{8}$$
$$\frac{6}{8} = \frac{3}{4}$$

$$1\frac{1}{9} =$$
$$-\frac{7}{9} =$$

$$1\frac{1}{7} =$$
$$-\frac{6}{7} =$$

$$1\frac{1}{12} =$$
$$-\frac{5}{12} =$$

$$1\frac{3}{5} =$$
$$-\frac{4}{5} =$$

$$1\frac{1}{6} =$$
$$-\frac{5}{6} =$$

69

Subtracting Fraction

Make necessary changes in the fractions and su
tract. Reduce your answers if necessary.

Here's how

$$1\frac{1}{12} = \frac{13}{12}$$
$$-\ \frac{1}{3} = \frac{4}{12}$$
$$\frac{9}{12} = \frac{3}{4}$$

$$1\frac{1}{8} =$$
$$-\ \frac{1}{2} =$$

$$1\frac{1}{8} =$$
$$-\ \frac{3}{4} =$$

$$1\frac{5}{8} =$$
$$-\ \frac{3}{4} =$$

$$1\frac{5}{6} =$$
$$-\ \frac{2}{3} =$$

$$1\frac{1}{10} =$$
$$-\ \frac{1}{2} =$$

70

Growing Up

The Bauer children measure themselves each year on January 1. Here are their measurements for two consecutive years. In the blank space at the bottom of the page or on your own paper, figure how much each child grew in one year.

Name	height / last year	this year	growth
Don	5′8½″	5′ 9⅛″	
Barbara	5′⅜″	5′1¼″	
Janice	4′10¾″	4′11⅜″	
Murray	4′6⅞″	4′7½″	
Lois	4′2″	4′5½″	
Kara	3′10½″	3′11¾″	

Don   Barbara   Janice

Keep going— on to step 5

Murray   Lois   Kara

You have finished

Step 4

71

Decimals

Find the sums and differences.

Decimals

Begin Step 5

3.6 +3.3 —— 6.9	4.2 +5.2	6.4 +1.4	3.1 +7.8
4.7 +3.2	4.9 +2.0	3.4 +1.2	8.2 +1.6
6.8 −2.6 —— 4.2	5.9 −3.2	6.7 −5.6	7.8 −2.5
5.8 −3.3	3.9 −1.5	5.8 −2.2	4.7 −3.4
3.4 +5.3	6.6 +1.2	4.7 −2.3	3.9 −2.7

The Homework Booklet

Decimals

Find the sums and differences.

.97 −.44	.74 −.43	.35 +.44	.16 +.22

6.73 +1.15	4.27 +5.52	3.46 +2.31

6.37 +3.52	5.47 +1.32	4.53 +2.41

9.97 −3.32	7.65 −4.21	2.98 −1.63

5.97 −2.84	9.87 −3.75	6.97 −4.76

73

Adding Decimal

Find pairs of numbers whose sum is 12.2

10	1.9	5.8	6.4	5.5
2.2	10.3	6.1	8.7	3.5
3.1	1.6	6.1	5	8.4
8.8	4.6	7.3	7.2	4.5
3.4	3.9	8	4.2	7.7

Also find pairs of numbers whose sum is 11.9.

Decimals

Find the sums and differences.

.236	.323	.546
+.821	+.845	+.853
1.057		

4.964	4.652	3.864
+3.753	+2.747	+1.117

.954	.652	.864
−.763	−.581	−.173

2.796	9.938	5.786
−1.385	−6.948	−3.493

5.879	8.879	6.854
−3.785	−2.892	+2.921

omework Booklet ©1983, Instructional Fair, Inc.

Decimal

Find the sums and differences.

3.25	3.82	4.73
5.73	4.15	2.49
+4.21	+2.38	+5.82

8.263	9.305	9.200
−3.352	−6.283	−3.032

9.975	6.895	1.589
−7.871	−4.174	−.306

3.441	4.214	3.564
6.567	2.389	6.038
+3.128	+6.463	+2.719

ecimals

Find the sums and differences.

14.5 −9.7	14.48 −13.49	7.23 +1.77
12.73 −5.283	17.001 −9.09	16.206 −5.359
8.463 .09 +9.263	7.25 16.305 +43.2	8.29 8.413 +9.326
18.152 −11.69	42.61 −32.6	17.9 −14.23
13.8 −6.9	9.23 −8.2	3.25 −.7

Number Tabl

Complete the table.

+	.3	.07		30	
				39	
.1	.4		5.1		
				50	
					.46
.8					1.2

The Homework Booklet

Number Sentences

Fill in the blanks so that all the number sentences are true.

					24
					+
20.1	+	7	=		
			—		=
	4.2	+	=		
=	+		=		
.4	50		7.1		
+	=				
	=		—	4.2	
				+	=
			10	+	2.5	=	
				=		—
.2	+		=			10.5

Working wit
Decima

Find the sums and differences.

26.2 −13.8	3.475 +12.5	9.33 −.43

9.33 6.231 +8.9	3.8 2.5 +23.7	14.865 24.8 +1.1

16.2 −7.893	6.005 +3.499	4.182 −3.295

15.01 .002 6.16 +35.213	3.152 .02 26.305 +14.003	4.27 1.002 .219 +27.106

umber Sentences

Il in the blanks so that all the numbers
ntences are true.

		—	8.3	=	4.0
		—			+
9.9	—	5.9	=		4.2
—			=		=
6.47	10	—		=	
=	—			—	
	6.5	3.6	—	.7	=
	=		=		—
	—		=		2.2
					=
	6.0	—		=	

Writing Decima
Problem

Copy and solve the following problems.

a. 73.695 + 44.38   f. 27.258 — 4.1

b. 29.263 — 24.35   g. 437.2 + 12.8

c. 49.363 — 28.7   h. 8.039 — 4.87

d. 5.245 + .763   i. 3.25 + 1.735

      e. .687 + 2.3

a.   73.695   b.   c.
+44.38

d.   e.   f.

g.   h.   i.

The Homework Booklet   ©1983, Instructional Fair, In

Jriting Decimal roblems

Copy and solve the following problems.

a. 9.038 + .003 + 7.305 + .35

b. 9.31 + 15.305 + 27.25 + 1.3

c. 3.25 + 1.730 + 8.3 + 42.1

d. 3.254 — .123   g. 1.76 — .157

e. 14.465 — .234   h. 4.97 + .435

f. 14.589 — 1.3067 i. 425.1 + .58

a.   b.   c.

d.   e.   f.

g.   h.   i.

Writing Decima
Problem

Copy and solve the following problems.

a. 14.036 — 4.341 d. 13.19 — 5.734

b. 13.066 — 4.214 e. 10.35 — 2.3844

c. 12.321 — 2.7   f. 13.04 — 1.001

g. 4.216 + .392 + 27.305 + 3.293

h. 13.26 + 2.905 + 9.7 + 46.258

i. 1.01 + .707 + 18.25 + 16.307

a. 14.036   b.   c.
  —4.341

d.   e.   f.

g.   h.   i.

The Homework Booklet   ©1983, Instructional Fair, Inc

nack Time

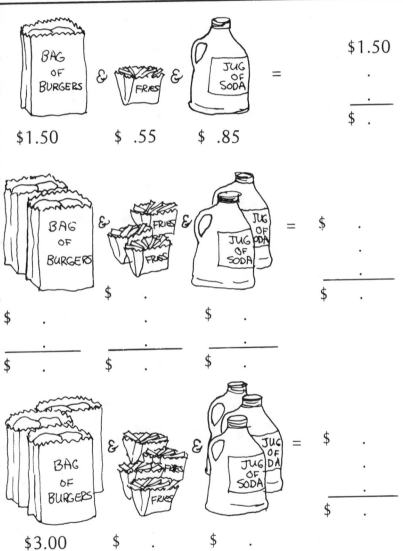

$1.50
.
.
—————
$.

$1.50 $ .55 $ .85

= $.
.
—————
$.

$. $. $.
.   .   .
—————   —————   —————
$. $. $.

= $.
.
.
—————
$.

$3.00 $. $.
.   .   .
—————   —————   —————
$. $. $.

What's for Supper

BUCKET OF CHICKEN & SALAD & GRAVY + POTATOES   = $3.

$3.50   .45 $ .50

$3.
+ .
+ .
‾‾‾‾‾
$.

& SALAD & GRAVY + POTATOES   = $.

$.

$. $. $.

$.   .   .

$. $. $.
‾‾‾‾   ‾‾‾‾   ‾‾‾‾

$.
‾‾‾‾
.

$.

You've earned your reward

You have finished this Book

& SALAD & GRAVY + POTATOES   = $.

$.

$7.00   . $.
+ .   .   .
‾‾‾‾   ‾‾‾‾   ‾‾‾‾
$. $. $.

$.
‾‾‾‾
$.

86